Designs That Sell

How To Make Your Home Show Better and Sell Faster

Gloria Hander Lyo.

Blue Sage Press

Designs That Sell
How To Make Your Home Show Better and Sell Faster

Copyright © 2007 by Gloria Hander Lyons

All Rights Reserved. No part of this book may be reproduced or utilized in any form or by any means, electronic or mechanical, including but not limited to photocopying, recording, or by any information storage and retrieval system without the prior written permission of the author.

Inquires should be addressed to:
Blue Sage Press
48 Borondo Pines
La Marque, TX 77568
www.BlueSagePress.com

ISBN: 978-0-9790618-7-5

Library of Congress Control Number: 2007907216

First Edition: October, 2007

The information in this book is true and complete to the best of our knowledge. All recommendations are made without guarantee on the part of the author or Blue Sage Press. The author and publisher disclaim any liability in connection with the use of this information.

Printed in the United States of America

Table of Contents

Introduction 1

Grab Them at the Curb 3
    Focus On Curb Appeal

Where's The House? 6
    Clear Out the Clutter

Fix It Up! 8
    Make Necessary Repairs

Use Your Nose 10
    Eliminate Unpleasant Odors

Tone It Down! 12
    Neutralize Your Home's Décor

The Emotion Quotient 14
    Depersonalize Your Home

Pet Control 15
    Managing Your Pets During Showings

Set the Stage 16
    Stimulate Your Buyer's Imagination

Wide Open Spaces 18
    Create a More Spacious Feel

The Arrangement 20
    Furniture Arranging Tips

What's the Point 23
    Creating Attractive Focal Points

Keep Things Light & Bright 27
    Proper Lighting To Show Off Your Home

Dress It Up 30
    Accessorizing Tips

Conflict or Harmony 35
    Creating an Inviting Space

Designer Tricks 39
    How To Camouflage Negative Features

A Little Bit of Money Can Get You a Lot More 42
    Investing in Home Improvements

That Empty Feeling 45
    Selling After You Move Out

The Latest Trends 46
    Make Your Home Compete in Today's Market

A Word About Professional Stagers 47
    Hiring a Professional to Help Stage Your Home

"Do-It-Yourself" Staging 49
    Easy Steps for Staging Your Home

The Virtual Tour 51
    On-line Home Shopping

A "Buyer's Eye" View 52
    Objective Assessment of Your Home's Condition

Introduction
Designs that Sell

When you decide to place your home on the market, there is a wise old saying you'll want to keep in mind: "You never get a second chance to make a first impression."

This is especially true when it comes time to show your home to prospective buyers. Making a good first impression can mean the difference between getting a quick sale with a great offer, or wasting valuable time showing your home month after month with no takers. It can also have a big impact on the final price you receive.

Every property will sell—eventually—if the price is low enough. But you've made a sizeable investment in your home, and you want a top-dollar return in the shortest time possible.

Investing a small amount of money and a little time and effort in home improvements and staging can give your house a solid advantage over your competition and reap big financial rewards.

Designs That Sell: How To Make Your Home Show Better and Sell Faster offers practical suggestions and decorating tips to make your property outshine all the others.

You'll learn helpful hints and creative ideas for furniture arranging, accessorizing, lighting, staging, de-cluttering, updating, how to use designer tricks and more.

Don't pass up the opportunity to impress potential buyers. All it takes is a small investment of time, money and effort to showcase your home's best features.

The suggestions offered in this simple step-by-step guide will help make your home show better and sell faster. Put them to work for you!

Grab Them at the Curb!

The very first impression any prospective buyer gets from your house is the outside view—also known as the "curb appeal". If buyers have a negative impression of your home's outside appearance, it can affect the way they will perceive the inside of your home as well. Some buyers might decide against going inside at all.

Make sure your house has positive curb appeal. If the outside of your home sparkles, potential buyers will be anxious to get inside. Focus on the following areas to make your house shine:

- Keep the grass well-watered and mowed. Have your trees trimmed. Cut back or replace overgrown shrubs. Plant a few blooming flowers to add color.

- Keep toys, bicycles, roller-skates, gardening equipment and other clutter stored away out of sight.

- Have the outside of your house painted, if needed. You want it to look brand new. Don't forget to paint or refinish the front door.

- Place a seasonal wreath on your front door to welcome buyers.

- Freshen up the front porch or entry. Put out a new doormat. Clean and polish the doorplate and doorknob.

- Make sure the door locks are in good working order and that the door opens smoothly to give real estate agents easy access.

- Paint the mailbox or replace it if it is not in good condition.

- Spruce up the light fixtures or add new ones if they are outdated.

- Make sure the house address numbers are neat and visible from the street.

- Sweep or pressure-wash the porch, driveway and front walkway. Check to see that these areas are in good repair, with no unsightly cracks or loose steps.

- Clean out and repair the gutters and downspouts.

- Repair or replace any loose or damaged shingles. You don't want potential buyers concerned about the cost of a new roof before they even get inside.

- Plant shrubs around a cable box or air conditioning unit to help disguise them.

- Install a low fence to hide the trash cans from view.

- Wash the windows and repair or replace any screens that are damaged or missing.

- If your garage doors take up a large portion of the front of your home, paint them a color that matches the exterior color of your home to help camouflage them. Paint the front door a complementary but contrasting color and spruce up the front entry with attractive plants to draw attention away from the garage doors.

- Make sure the back yard and side yards look as good as the front. Just because they are hidden behind a fence doesn't mean you can neglect them. Buyers will inspect these areas, as well.

- After dark, turn on your front porch light and any other exterior lighting to create a warm and welcoming feel.

Your overall objective is to project an attractive, well-maintained image that will welcome prospective buyers into your home.

Paying attention to these details can make a big difference in the overall impression your home has on buyers.

Where's the House?

Would you purchase a home you can't see?

- Is your home is crowded with too much furniture?
- Are the closets and cabinets are overflowing?
- Are your kitchen and bathroom countertops loaded with clutter?
- Do you have lots of family photos or collectibles on display?

If your home suffers from any or all of the above, then potential buyers won't be able to see your home. They will be overwhelmed by the chaos and wonder what else might be hiding underneath all the clutter.

Before putting your home on the market, get rid of anything you don't absolutely need or use. This means you'll need to sort through all your belongings and divide them into categories of things to toss out, things to sell or donate and things to keep.

And don't forget about all that stuff piled up in the garage. Buyers will need to inspect this area, as well, so make sure they have easy access.

This de-cluttering process will take some time and effort, but the result will make your home more attractive to buyers. It will also lighten your load considerably when it comes time to pack up and move.

After getting rid of your excess baggage, make sure all the items you decide to keep are neatly organized and stored away.

If you can't bear to part with any of your possessions, then get a head start on your packing. Box up all your stuff and rent an off-site storage space to store it while showing your home.

Clutter creates a feeling of chaos and stress. Our homes should be a comfortable haven from the hectic world outside. By removing the excess stuff from your closets and cabinets, clearing off your countertops and moving out unnecessary furniture and accessories, you will be able to present an orderly, serene and spacious environment to buyers.

So, box up the clutter and move it out!

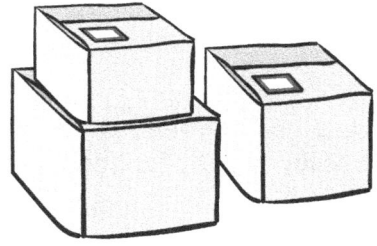

Fix It Up!

Take note of any necessary repairs that need to be made before you place your home on the market. Buyers expect everything in their new home to operate safely and properly.

Most buyers will notice any minor maintenance problems that you have left unattended. Make sure your property is in top-notch condition.

- Repair leaky faucets in the kitchen or bathrooms.

- Check to see that the sinks, tubs and showers drain well and toilets are in good working order.

- Clean and repair windows that are painted-shut or have cracked or broken panes.

- Clean the furnace and air conditioning filters and vents.

- Replace old caulk around tubs, showers and sinks and remove any signs of mildew.

- Clean soap scum or mineral deposits from glass shower doors and replace shower curtain liners that show signs of mildew or stains.

- Clean and repair kitchen appliances and make sure they are working properly.

- Repair or replace kitchen or bathroom countertops that are scratched, stained or chipped.

- Paint or refinish kitchen or bathroom cabinets that are scuffed, damaged or outdated.

- Repair cracked plaster in walls or ceilings. Fill any nail holes and give all the walls a fresh coat of paint if needed.

- Oil squeaking doors and adjust doors that stick.

- Repair squeaking floor boards and stair treads.

- Clean or replace worn or stained carpets.

- Repair or replace scratched or worn vinyl floors or cracked or chipped ceramic tile floors.

These repairs may seem small, but if left undone, they can lead buyers to question whether you've taken good care of your home. They might also wonder what other, more serious problems might have been neglected.

Don't give your prospective buyers an excuse to start tallying up repair costs that will be deducted from the final sale price.

Use Your Nose

After living in our homes for years, we become accustomed to odors that others might find offensive. To eliminate bad smells that could send your buyers running, consider the following tips:

- Bathe your pets and freshen the cat litter box frequently.

- Shampoo your carpets to eliminate any odors absorbed into the fibers.

- If weather permits, open the windows and let in some fresh air

- Dry clean your draperies and clean the window blinds or shades.

- Empty trash cans frequently. No one wants to buy a home that smells like last week's garbage.

- Eliminate any mildew smells in bathrooms. Mold and mildew can be signs of plumbing problems and potential repair bills.

- Avoid cooking strong-smelling food during times when your home might be shown.

- Baking a homemade or frozen pie or cookies is a good way to make your home smell more inviting.

- Clean any messy food spills or stains off the countertops, stove, oven and refrigerator.

- Turn on the air conditioner or central heating units to keep air circulating throughout the home and eliminate that "stuffy" smell.

- Introduce pleasing smells by placing flowers or potpourri in your home, but beware of using strong-smelling air fresheners. Buyers might wonder what odor you are trying to hide.

Don't give buyers a reason to turn up their noses after getting a whiff of your property. Make sure your home smells fresh, clean and new.

Tone It Down!

Since you have no idea what the decorating tastes of your buyers might be, you will need to tone down the level of your home's décor in order to make it agreeable to most people. The key is to avoid eccentric décor.

- Paint the walls a neutral color (avoid stark white) throughout your home. Light-colored, neutral hues can create the illusion of larger rooms and give your home a fresh, clean, updated look.

- Remove dated or flamboyant wallpaper. Freshly painted walls are always more appealing to buyers than the prospect of stripping wallpaper.

- Try to neutralize the décor in your living spaces by removing unusual artwork or eccentric paintings that some buyers might find offensive.

- Tone down the décor in your kids' rooms by removing wild teenage posters, toddler-themed wall murals or scary reptile pets.

- Remove any decorative items that might be offensive or distracting, like stuffed animal-head trophies or 1960's-style beaded doorway curtains.

- Reduce the number of accessories to a minimum, and remove any large collections of objects in order to present a clean, uncluttered look.

- Remove fussy or flamboyant window treatments that might make the room feel dark or outdated.

- Replace carpets that might be classified as an extreme color or pattern choice with ones that most buyers will consider "move-in-ready".

- Choose a decorating style that has a simple, clean look that will appeal to a broad range of people.

Potential buyers want to see your house, not your personal decorating style. Get rid of anything that might distract them or worse, send them running out the door in panic.

The Emotion Quotient

When you place your house on the market, it's no longer your home, it's a property to be sold. And remember, your goal is to snag a quick sale for the highest possible price. Therefore, you need to remove your "emotional" possessions—all those items you have collected over the years that represent ties to you and your memories.

Depersonalize your home by removing collections of family photographs, souvenirs, trophies, refrigerator magnets, etc. These items not only make your space feel cluttered, they distract buyers.

You want your buyers to focus on the layout of the home and its architectural features—not the clutter. They might also find it difficult to imagine their own possessions in a home that is filled with your memorabilia.

Get a head start on your packing and box up all your personal mementos and treasures, then store them out of sight.

Pet Control

Many people have allergies and/or concerns when it comes to animals. If you have a pet, make arrangements to have it elsewhere when your home is being shown. If you must keep your pet at home, consider the following advice:

- Don't lock your pet in one of the rooms in your home, so buyers can't view that area, but do confine pets so they can't attack (friendly or otherwise) potential buyers.

- Keep your pet's feeding dishes out of sight.

- Make sure all floors and furniture are "pet-hair" free.

- Clean litter boxes frequently.

- Shampoo your pets frequently.

- Shampoo your carpets to remove pet odors.

- If weather permits, open the windows to air out your home.

- Make sure outside pets are contained in an area that will allow buyers to inspect the backyard.

Set the Stage

Staging a property for sale is a way to stimulate the buyer's imagination about what it would feel like to live in your home. You want to create vignettes throughout the house that will make buyers want to linger in the space and imagine themselves living there.

Set the stage by appealing to their emotions through sights, sounds and smells.

- Create a warm and inviting display in the entry, such as a framed mirror over a small table with a vase of fresh flowers that says, "Welcome home."

- Set the dining room table with your best dishes so buyers can imagine themselves entertaining friends and family in the space.

- Put out fluffy white towels, scented soaps and candles in the bathrooms to create a look that says, "Come in and relax."

- Add attractive new bedding in your bedrooms if your current bedding is looking a bit shabby or outdated. Use neutral or low-key colors to create a soothing retreat for new homeowners.

- Hang new curtains that make your room look fresh and airy. A simple valance over sheer curtains or blinds will present a cleaner, lighter feel.

- Light some logs in the fireplace if the season allows, which will create a warm, inviting atmosphere.

- Leave an open cookbook on the kitchen counter and fill the room with the aroma of baking cookies or apple pie.

- Place a pitcher of lemonade on a table on the back porch or patio. Add a couple of comfy patio chairs to make buyers long for a relaxing break outside.

When staging your property for sale, create a homey feel for buyers.

Wide Open Spaces

Creating an open, spacious feeling in your home will help convince prospective buyers that they are getting a good value for their real estate dollars.

The following tips will help achieve your goal to make your living space seem larger:

- Make sure all doors, cabinets and drawers open all the way without bumping into furniture or getting snagged on contents jammed inside. You don't want to create the impression that the rooms are too small or you have insufficient storage space.

- Clear all clutter and/or appliances off your kitchen and bathroom countertops. Clean out and organize inside drawers, cabinets and pantries. Buyers usually inspect these areas.

- Avoid placing large pieces of furniture close to the entrance into a room, which creates a road block. Arrange the furniture so it welcomes buyers into the space. See the sample layouts on pages 20-22.

- Make sure there is enough room for people to walk through the rooms comfortably without bumping into furniture. Traffic paths should be about three feet wide if possible.

- Limit the number of task areas in each room, such as home office/bedroom or bedroom/exercise room, to prevent overcrowding the space and causing confusion among buyers about the room's purpose. Even if you currently use your formal dining room as an office, show it as a dining room so buyers will have no doubt about its function.

- Clean out the clutter in all your closets. Now is the time to toss unnecessary items or have a garage sale to get rid of anything you don't need. Pack up your out-of-season clothing and store it out of sight or at an off-site storage facility. You want all your storage areas to appear roomy and spacious.

- Move oversized furniture to a storage facility. Having too much furniture in a room or using furniture that is too large in scale will make the room seem smaller. Don't give buyers any reason to feel your home is too small for their belongings.

Focus on creating a sense of spaciousness in all the rooms in your home. Avoid crowding your space with too much furniture and arrange the pieces to promote easy traffic flow. Clear out all the closets and storage areas to make them seem larger. Buyers will feel they are getting more space for their money.

The Arrangement

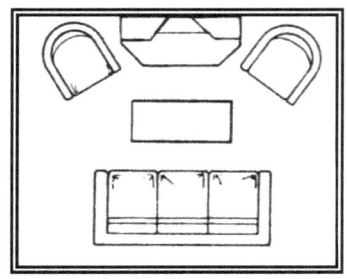

When staging your home for potential buyers, it's important to create attractive furniture layouts to make your rooms look their best. A few tips are listed below that might be helpful:

1. Avoid pushing all the furniture in your living room up against the walls, leaving a huge empty space in the middle of the room. If space allows, arrange your conversation area furniture into a smaller, more functional group in the center of the room. You will create a more spacious feel and allow for traffic to flow around the conversation area as shown in Figure 1 below.

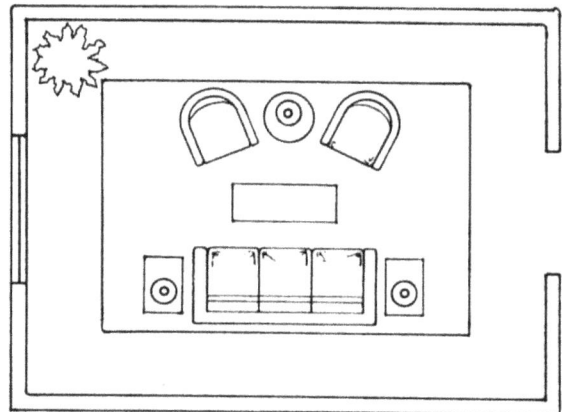

Figure 1

2. Try placing your furniture on the diagonal instead of square with the walls. Arranging the conversation area diagonally in your room can add a sense of motion. Repeating this angle by placing other furniture pieces on the diagonal will create continuity. See Figure 2 below.

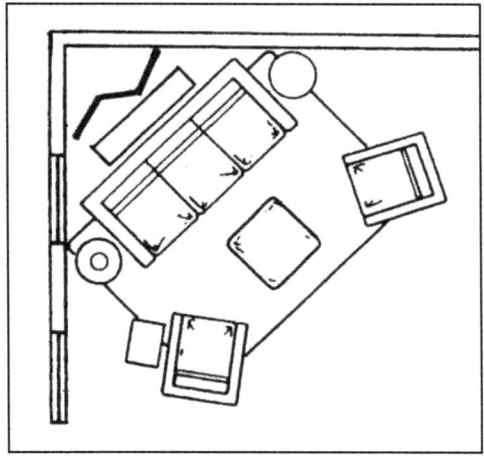

Figure 2

In this example, the sofa is placed on an angle in the corner in front of a standing screen and a sofa table for displaying accessories. This arrangement creates the focal point of the room, since the space has no prominent architectural feature.

The sofa is flanked by an end table on the right and a floor lamp on the left. The chairs, as well as the area rug, are also placed on an angle. This arrangement creates a welcoming entrance that draws buyers into the room.

3. If the room is a long, rectangular shape, divide it into two separate activity areas, such as reading, watching television, or sitting by the fire. See Figure 3 below.

On the left side of the room, two wing-back chairs were arranged in front of the fireplace for a relaxing place to read or enjoy the fire. A lamp was added to the table in between the two chairs for lighting.

There is a comfortable conversation area on the right side of the room, placed on an angle to create a more welcoming approach from the room's entrance. An entertainment center was included in this area for watching television. Both seating groups were anchored with area rugs to help define the separate spaces.

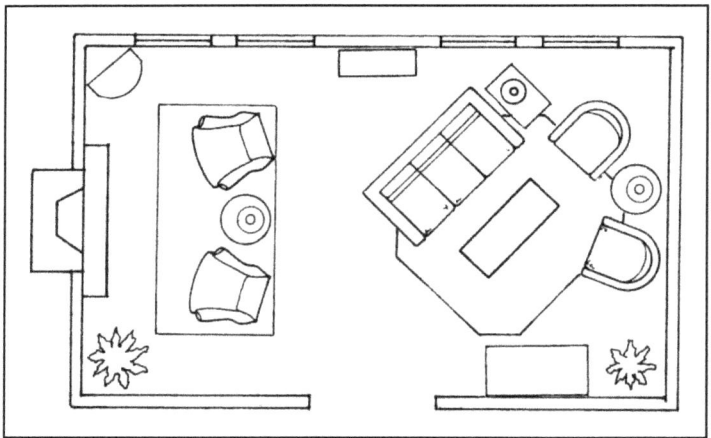

Figure 3

Try arranging the furniture in your rooms to create an open feel that invites your buyers to come in and enjoy the space.

What's the Point?

When preparing your home for sale, make an effort to highlight a prominent architectural feature or create an attractive vignette on one of the walls in each room, which can serve as the room's focal point.

The focal point can be a fireplace with decorations above the mantel, a window with a nice view or artwork arranged over a sofa.

If you have a room with a beautiful view, make it the focal point of your room. Arrange the furniture to draw attention toward it. Frame the window with drapery panels or fabric swags and position a tall plant or topiary on either side of the window to help make it stand out.

If the fireplace is an attractive architectural feature in your living room, orient your furniture toward it. Arrange a group of accessories, such as framed mirrors, paintings, vases, candles and other objects on or over the mantle in order to create a pleasing composition that will attract your buyer's attention.

Try to make the composition large enough in scale and extended high enough on the wall above the mantel shelf to establish its importance. A good example is a large painting hung above the mantel shelf, in the center, and two identical candlesticks placed on either side of the painting. See Figure 4 below.

Figure 4

Figure 5

You can also create a more casual arrangement from a group of objects of varying sizes and shapes, such as a large framed mirror placed on the mantel shelf, slightly off center, which is balanced by a vase filled with a tall floral arrangement, as shown in Figure 5 above.

Painting an accent wall in a darker or more vibrant color is another way to make your focal point stand out. For example, if your focal point is a fireplace which has a white mantle shelf and wood trim, and your room is painted a neutral beige color, then painting the wall that the fireplace is on with a darker shade of beige (or one of your accent colors in the room, such as blue) will draw the eye to that wall. It will also make the fireplace "pop" because of the white paint of the wood trim against the darker wall color.

If you don't have a fireplace in your living room, you can create a focal point by arranging decorative objects and artwork over a sofa or an attractive piece of furniture, such as a chest or entry table. See the example below.

Painting an accent wall in a contrasting color behind these arrangements will also create more impact for your focal point.

There are many other possibilities for creating focal points in your rooms. In the dining room, you can arrange decorative plates on the wall above a sideboard, as shown at right.

For the bedroom, you might gather curtain panels onto a rod and hang them on the wall behind the headboard.

Create a focal point in each of your rooms, whether it's a prominent architectural feature, a window with an attractive view or an arrangement of artwork over a piece of furniture for your potential buyers to admire.

Keep Things Light and Bright

A lot of natural or artificial light in a room gives it an open and airy feel. It also makes a room feel more spacious. The following tips will help brighten your home:

- Replace bulbs that don't work and use as much wattage as is appropriate for each fixture.

- Remember to balance the light throughout the room using a variety of fixtures such as table lamps, floor lamps, wall sconces and accent lights.

- For showings, turn on lights in every room.

- Remove heavy draperies that might make a room feel dark or outdated. A simple valance over sheer curtains or blinds will present a cleaner, lighter feel.

- Address any dark corners in your rooms by adding a floor lamp, a lamp on a table or a floor can behind a tall plant.

- Open the blinds (which, of course, are dust free) to let in more light, and make sure the window panes are squeaky clean.

- Replace dark or opaque lampshades with lighter colored, translucent ones, which give off more light.

- Clean the glass globes or shades on all light fixtures, sconces and chandeliers.

- Remove window screens—they block natural light. This also opens the view to the outside and expands the visual space in the room.

When planning for lighting in your rooms, be sure to provide adequate light for tasks such as reading or deskwork. Table lamps and floor lamps are good choices for task lighting. Be sure to distribute them evenly throughout the space for more balanced lighting.

There should also be enough general (or ambient) lighting in the room to prevent it from being too dark. Use fixtures such as chandeliers, torchieres (floor lamps that shine light upward), sconces and track lights for general lighting.

The lighting you choose for your room greatly affects the mood. A brightly lit room projects a more work oriented mood, such as the light needed in a kitchen. A dimly lit room is more intimate and romantic, such as the level of light desirable in a bedroom or formal dining room. Decide what lighting mood you want to stage in each room in order to show off your home to its best advantage, just remember to keep the level of light bright enough for buyers to see the space.

Keep in mind that the light fixtures you select express a certain style. Some fixtures, such as table lamps, chandeliers and sconces, are more traditional and some are more contemporary in style. Some are lavish and ornate; others are simple and stark.

As with the furniture you selected, lighting fixtures should complement the style of your décor. For example, a modern chandelier would not be suitable in mood or style for a Victorian dining room.

You can also provide accents of light in specific areas of a room to add a dramatic touch. This type of lighting is called accent lighting. A few examples are listed below:

- Use a floor can to shine light up through the foliage of a large plant.

- Showcase a piece of art using a picture light or wall-washer (either ceiling mounted or portable floor light that shines light onto the walls).

- Use low-voltage rope lights (tiny lights inside a flexible plastic tube) on top of kitchen wall cabinets to provide indirect lighting.

- Use a lamp on a table to brighten a dark corner.

- Use rope lights behind each curtain valance to provide a pleasant glow at night and highlight the fabric of the draperies in your room.

Accent lighting not only highlights special artwork and brightens dark corners, it adds drama and interest to your décor. Plan your lighting carefully to make your home sparkle.

Designer Trick: Windowpane mirrors (wall art that looks like a window frame with a mirror behind it) or even a group of framed mirrors can create the illusion of real windows on a windowless wall, reflecting light into the space, as well as adding architectural interest to the room.

Dress It Up

For showing your home, you want to keep accessories to a minimum, but they can certainly add to the overall appeal. The following guidelines for accessorizing will help you stage beautiful displays throughout your home.

Wall Art

Accessories add warmth and interest to a room. Wall art, such as paintings, prints, tapestries, framed mirrors and even three dimensional objects such as sculptures, metalwork and sconces are an important part of the room's décor; therefore, it's important to display them properly.

One of the most common decorating mistakes is hanging artwork too high, so that it appears to be "floating" by itself on the wall. It should be hung low enough so it is viewed as part of a grouping of furniture and other objects beneath it.

When hanging a piece of art over a sofa, it should be hung only about eight to ten inches above the sofa back.

Figure 6 on page 31 shows an example of "floating" art. Compare it to Figure 7.

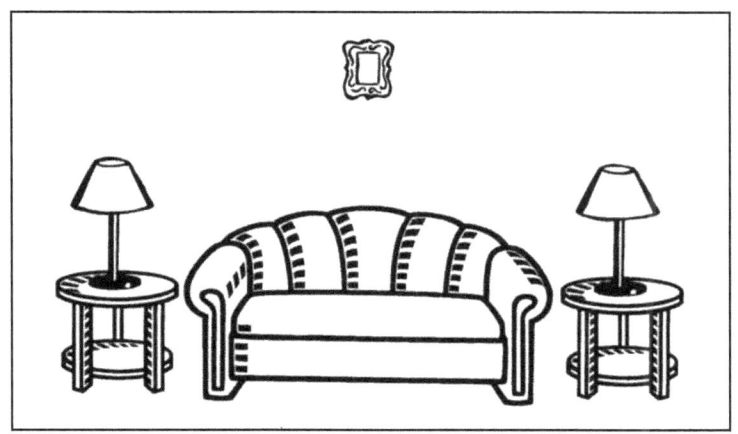

Figure 6

Figure 7

Wall art can help establish the focal point of a room. A focal point should create sufficient impact to draw your attention, such as a large framed mirror hung over a chest of drawers in the foyer or a painting hung over the fireplace mantel.

When hanging a large piece of wall art, check to see that its scale and shape are a good fit for the space where it will be hung. For example, the shape of the wall space above a sofa is usually a horizontal, rectangular shape. Therefore, the best shape for artwork to fit this space is a rectangular or oval shape, hung horizontally. If the wall space is square, use a square or round piece of artwork. The art in Figure 6 is not an appropriate shape for this space.

Next, check the size of the wall art. Does it appear to be too large for the scale of the sofa, or is it too small to create the impact you want? The art piece in Figure 6 is too small in scale for the size of this sofa. If you don't have one piece of artwork that is large enough, use several smaller pieces in a grouping.

When arranging a group of framed prints or paintings, hang them close enough together so they appear to be one unit, but not so close that the space looks crowded. There is no magic formula for determining how far apart to place the artwork because it varies according to the size of the pieces. Just stand back and take a good look. Does the spacing feel right or does it need to be adjusted? Does the scale of the overall grouping fit the space you need to fill?

It's usually a good idea to choose a similar frame material for all the pictures in the grouping—gold, silver, wood, lacquer, etc. And take note of the frame styles, whether they are rustic, contemporary, traditional, etc. Do they fit with the style of the other furnishings in your room?

Accessories for the Room

The other category for accessories includes items such as vases, throw pillows, sculptures, plants, candelabras, framed photographs and clocks which are placed on the floor, tables, shelves or sofas and chairs.

Keep these accessories to a minimum; you don't want a cluttered look. Your potential buyers need to focus on your home—not your décor.

Avoid scattering small accessories around the room. This makes the space feel cluttered. Instead, group small objects, such as baskets or vases, together in one display to create more of an impact. But make sure the items you display are suitable in mood and style for the room.

> Designer Tip: If you want an object to stand out, place it against a sharply contrasting color background. A dark object on a white shelf will be more visible and draw more attention. If you want to camouflage an object (such as a piece of furniture that is too large for the space), place it in front of a similar colored background.

Don't forget to address any empty corners in your room. You might want to soften the sharpness of a corner by using accessories. Some possibilities are a tall potted plant or a lamp on a table. Another option is a tall decorative folding screen.

Try to balance the soft and hard materials in your room. Too many hard surfaces will make the space feel cold and uninviting. Use fabrics, plants, rugs, pillows, etc. to add some softness and warmth.

Window treatments help soften the hard, rectangular lines of windows and enhance the room's décor. Keep them simple and make sure they complement the color and decorating style you have chosen for the room.

Area rugs are accessories for the floor. They add color, texture and design patterns to your room. They can also help define a conversation area and cover cold, bare floors to make a room feel more cozy.

Keep in mind that when accessorizing your home for sale, you want to create beautiful displays to make the rooms feel more inviting, but at the same time you don't want the space to feel cluttered or cramped.

Conflict or Harmony

A very important goal when staging your home for sale is to create a sense of harmony in your rooms. This means that all the décor in the room (every piece of furniture, every accessory, every window treatment and wall covering) should harmonize with the overall color scheme and furniture style you have chosen to stage for potential buyers.

Make sure that each piece of furniture you use is suitable in mood and style for the décor. If the decorating style is contemporary and you plan to use sleek, modern furniture, then an ornate Victorian table would not be suitable for the room. Choose a decorating style that will appeal to most buyers. Keep it clean, simple and uncluttered. Buyers should be able to focus on the home and its architectural features—not your furniture.

Choose accessories that are appropriate to the room's décor, as well. Don't display rustic, country pottery on a modern fireplace mantle. Use accessories in moderation, and remember to remove personal items, like framed photos or portraits or keep them to a minimum.

Balance is also an essential element for creating harmony in a room. Whether referring to the placement of furniture, color or lighting, it is important to distribute them evenly throughout the space, or the room will feel off balance.

The furniture layout in Figure 8 below shows an example of an even distribution of furniture in a living room. The sofa and two club chairs are pulled into a tight group to form a comfortable conversation area. The group is oriented toward the fireplace, which is the focal point of this room. The homeowners have left ample space for traffic to flow around the furniture. They did not place any furniture close to the entrances into the room, which might create a road block for traffic flow.

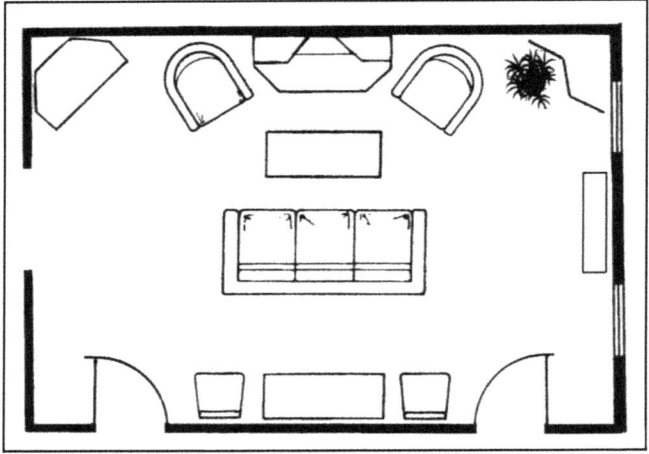

Figure 8

In addition to distributing your furniture evenly throughout the space, also check for balance among the heights of the major furniture pieces. This doesn't mean that all the furniture pieces should be the same height. You want a mixture of tall and low objects to provide more interest.

Simply check to see that the taller pieces are dispersed evenly. If you have a tall piece of furniture on one wall, balance it on the opposite wall with another tall piece, or a shorter piece of furniture with artwork arranged above it to create enough visual weight to balance the taller piece.

Another important aspect to consider when selecting the furniture for your room is scale. Scale refers to the size of a piece of furniture in relation to the size of the other furniture in the room, or in relation to the size of the room itself. For example, a giant sofa in a tiny room is out of scale with the room. Large dining chairs crowded around a small dining table are out of scale with the table.

The easiest way to keep all the furniture in your room in scale is to start by choosing the most important piece first, such as the sofa for a living room or the dining table for a dining room. If you make sure that this piece is in scale with the room, and check carefully that all the other pieces of furniture are in scale with this piece, then you will have harmony in scale for the entire room.

Select pieces of furniture that fit with the style of your décor and are in scale with the size of each room in order to achieve a harmonious design and make your home feel more spacious.

Using pairs of objects creates symmetry, which helps give the room a balanced look. Even with only three pieces in a display, a pair of things (such as two candlesticks) flanking a large object (such as a vase) will make a pleasing composition, as shown in the example below.

Another example of symmetry is a pair of matching table lamps on either end of a sofa, as shown in Figure 7 on page 31. Remember to keep your décor simple and orderly to appeal to most buyers.

When decorating a bookcase, use the "one-third" rule: one third books, one third accessories and one third space. Don't overcrowd the shelves or it will look cluttered.

Repeating a color, shape or pattern at least three times in a room helps to provide continuity. Whether it is a type of metal finish, a fabric print or a geometric shape, try to repeat it several times throughout the space.

If the drawer pulls on your cabinetry are bronze, repeat that same finish in the lamp bases and accessories around the room. Another example is using the same fabric from your window treatments in accent pillows on your upholstered chairs or a tablecloth on a side table.

Creating a sense of harmony in your decorating scheme will make your home more appealing to buyers.

Designer Tricks

Pay attention to any positive or negative architectural features in your home that you might want to accentuate or camouflage. If your rooms have distinctive crown moldings, you might paint or stain them a contrasting color to draw attention to them. If you have an attractive fireplace, make it a focal point by adding an arrangement of artwork over it, highlight it with accent lighting and orient the furniture in the room to focus in that direction.

Use some of the following designer tricks to camouflage negative architectural features:

To make a small room feel larger:

- Use small-scale furniture in the room.
- Use solid color upholstery fabrics or fabrics with small design motifs.
- Avoid crowding the room with too much furniture.
- Paint the walls a light, neutral color and try to unify the space by painting doors and trim the same color as the walls.
- The window treatment color should blend, not contrast, with the wall color.
- Don't break up the floor space with area rugs.

To make a low ceiling appear higher:

- Use the principal of vertical lines by removing any horizontal moldings or paint them the same color as the walls.

- Window treatments should continue from floor to ceiling to avoid cutting the vertical height.

- Paint the ceiling a light color (white is best) to make it appear to recede.

- A darker floor color makes floors appear lower than they actually are.

To make a narrow room feel wider:

- Paint the end walls a darker color and use a light color on the long walls.

- Use a striped rug with the stripes running across the width.

- In a long, narrow hallway, avoid hanging art on the side walls, instead hang a framed print or other wall art at the far end.

Changing the appearance of windows:

If a window appears to be too short, add a valance above the window where the bottom of the valance starts just below the top edge of the window, and the top of the valance extends above the window to make the window appear much taller. See Figure 9 on page 41.

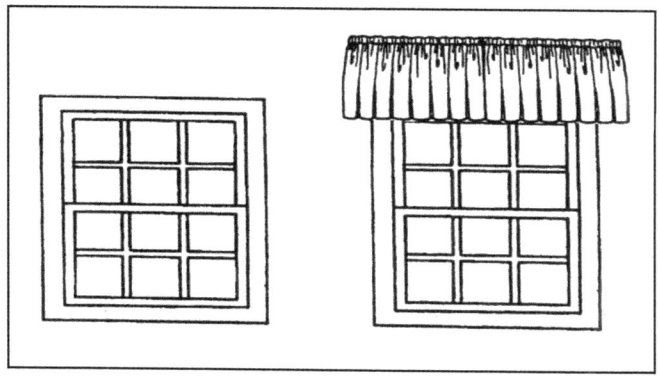

Figure 9

If a window appears to be too narrow, add curtain panels to each side of the window, which start at the sides of the window and extend onto the wall on either side, making it appear wider. See Figure 10 below.

Figure 10

Designer Tip: If you want to camouflage an object (such as a piece of furniture that is too large for the space), place it in front of a similar colored background.

A Little Bit of Money Can Get You a Lot More

Some sellers are hesitant to invest money in their homes before putting them on the market. In most cases, however, spending one or two thousand dollars to update your property is a good investment.

As long as you stay within a reasonable remodeling budget, you should be able to more than recoup your costs, and the improvements usually result in a quicker sale, as well as a higher selling price. Your real estate agent should be able to offer guidance about any specific projects you are considering.

Most buyers want a house that is move-in ready. With a little time, money and effort, your house can be, too. And if you're handy, you can save on costs by doing most of the work yourself. It will be well worth your time.

Below is a list of some areas that you might want to address:

- Paint or have the entire house painted both inside and out. Your house will look and feel brand new.

- Replace stained or worn carpets—at least in the larger public areas such as the family room, but preferably any rooms that would make a buyer start to tally the replacement costs himself.

- Refinish hardwood floors if they are scuffed or damaged.

- Replace worn, scratched or peeling vinyl floors or cracked or chipped ceramic tile floors.

- Replace light fixtures that are insufficient, broken, discolored or outdated—especially those in the kitchen, dining room, breakfast room and bathrooms.

- Consider replacing severely outdated kitchen appliances, as long as you stay within a reasonable price range.

- Replace faucets in the kitchen or bathrooms that are corroded, tarnished, leaky or outdated.

- If your bathroom or kitchen cabinets are dark, discolored or outdated, paint them—preferably in a light color or white. To do this, remove all the cabinet doors. Clean all cabinet surfaces with a solution of water and detergent. Let them dry and lightly sand all surfaces. Remove any dust with a damp cloth, let dry and prime all surfaces with primer suitable for covering the previous finish type (enamel, stain, latex—consult with the paint expert at your local home improvement store). Let dry and paint all surfaces with latex or enamel paint, whichever product is appropriate for your project.

- Replace the handles and drawer pulls on your kitchen and bathroom cabinets. This is a quick, inexpensive change that can make a big difference in updating the look.

- If your bathroom or kitchen countertops are scratched, stained or chipped, consider replacing them with new laminate countertops, which are fairly inexpensive. Keep your color choices in the neutral zone. If you're handy at tiling, you can replace the countertops with ceramic tile for very little cost and a big return on your time and money.

- If your furniture is worn, stained or outdated, consider buying new slip covers for the upholstered pieces and refinishing the wooden pieces. If you don't plan to use your current furniture in your new home and don't want to spend money updating it, get rid of it and buy, borrow or rent just enough attractive pieces to stage your home while it's on the market.

- Replace dingy, outdated bedding and window treatments, but avoid bright colors and bold prints. Keep your new choices in the neutral tone range that will appeal to most buyers.

Investing a little time, effort and money in sprucing up your property before showing it to prospective buyers can net you a faster sale at a higher price.

That Empty Feeling

If you need to move out before your home is sold, try to leave a few items behind to stage some of the rooms for showing. A furnished home usually sells faster than a vacant one.

Even if you have just a few pieces of furniture in some of the rooms, such as a chair, an end table and a lamp in the living room to suggest a purpose for the room, it's better than the hollow, cold sound of empty space. Empty rooms also seem smaller than furnished rooms.

Plan to stage a few rooms with furniture you might not need in your new home. If you don't have any furniture to spare, pick up a few pieces at garage sales or flea markets, or borrow them from friends, family or neighbors.

Just make sure the pieces you plan to use are attractive and in good condition. Then create a cozy vignette in several rooms to make them feel more inviting.

The Latest Trends

When marketing your home, it's important to be aware of what's "hot" with buyers in the current market.

One of the latest trends in homes today is the media room—a room designed specifically for watching movies on a big screen television. You might consider rearranging the furniture in what was previously a game room or den to look more like a media room, which could make it more appealing to buyers.

Many young buyers today feel that a formal living room is wasted space. In order to create a more updated feel that will appeal to these buyers, reconfigure your formal living room as a home office.

In this age of rapidly advancing computer technology, when many people work from their homes, almost every family needs a home office. Consider staging one of your bedrooms as an office instead of a bedroom.

Visit model homes in your area to stay abreast of new trends that are popular with buyers so you can keep your property competitive in today's market.

A Word About Professional Stagers

Most homeowners should be able to get their property into good saleable shape just by following the tips presented in this book. However, if you don't feel that you have the time or skills to accomplish the desired results, you might investigate the possibility of hiring a professional home stager.

Your real estate agent should be able to recommend a reputable home staging consultant in your area, or you can search for companies online that offer home staging services. Make sure to get references for any company you are considering.

Will the outcome be worth the money invested? Visit a few homes on the market in your area to do a bit of comparison shopping. If those properties show better than your home, that's a good sign that you need to invest some time and effort in home improvements and staging.

Real estate agents should consider offering the services of a professional stager as part of their marketing package, even if it's just for a one hour pre-listing consultation. Home staging is an added-value marketing service that will increase the perceived value of your home to help it show better and sell more quickly. Most sellers would prefer to hire a realtor who offers professional home-staging services than one who doesn't.

Staging services can range from de-cluttering to rearranging the existing furnishings and accessories to completely refurnishing the entire home. Whatever degree of staging you do can make a significant difference in selling your home.

Some realtors recommend spending one-half of one percent of the asking price for staging. Depending on the staging consultant, it can cost much less, but the money spent on staging can actually increase the final sale price of your home.

Effective staging appeals to buyers' emotions and creates an atmosphere that makes them want to linger and imagine themselves living in the space.

Whether you stage your home yourself or hire a consultant, creating a feeling of spaciousness and hominess can help sell your house faster and increase your overall profit.

"Do-It-Yourself" Staging

By using the general decorating guidelines described in this book, you should be able to stage the interior spaces of your home to make them more appealing. Follow the steps listed below to complete each room:

1. Start with a clean slate by removing everything from the room, if possible. Since you're planning to move soon, this would be a good time to pack up and move out any items you don't need.

2. Check the condition of the walls to see if any repairs need to be made. Then decide if you need to paint the room, or perhaps just paint an accent wall. Remember, you want your home to look fresh and new, and keep the colors a light, neutral shade.

3. Decide on the function of your room so potential buyers will have a clear idea about the room's purpose. Scour your entire house to find the furniture pieces you will need to set the stage. Make sure all furniture is in good condition and fits the style of décor you have chosen for the space.

4. Arrange the furniture in the room, following the decorating guidelines for balance, traffic patterns and general layout. Use furniture sparingly—don't overcrowd the space. You want to have an open feel and easy traffic flow in each room.

5. Create a focal point in each room that draws your buyers' attention as soon as they enter. Whether it is the fireplace with attractive decorations above the mantel, a window with a beautiful view that is framed with curtain panels, or artwork arranged over a sofa, create an interesting vignette for your buyers to admire.

6. Remove any heavy or outdated window coverings and try to find creative but inexpensive treatments that will harmonize with the new decorating scheme. Keep them simple, such as straight, full-length panels on each side of the window, or a fabric swag or valance over sheer curtains or blinds.

7. Add the appropriate lighting to make your room sparkle. You will need general lighting to light the overall room, task lighting for specific areas, and accent lighting to brighten dark corners and highlight special artwork on walls or shelves. Be sure the lighting is balanced throughout the space.

8. Accessorize your room using the suggestions listed previously. Search your home for any accessories that would be suitable in style and color for your new spaces. Don't forget area rugs, pillows, throws, framed prints or mirrors, plants, and anything else you might find to create interesting displays. But don't overdo the accessories. You want to avoid a cluttered look.

Set the stage to give your home a comfortable, spacious and inviting feel—one that will make buyers want to live there.

The Virtual Tour

Making the effort to prepare your home for sale not only helps your home show better and sell faster when potential buyers are touring the property in person, but also when they are "shopping" for houses online.

Using today's computer technology and the Internet, buyers can pull up a list of homes that meet their criteria and take a virtual tour of the listings without ever leaving their chairs.

Online house shopping eliminates a lot of legwork, as well as time, because buyers can compare photos of all the properties on their list and decide which ones are worth visiting with their real estate agents.

It's important to get your home in good shape before the listing photos are taken for the real estate websites. These photos are the very first impressions online buyers will get of your home, so make sure your property outshines all the others.

A "Buyer's-Eye" View

Before planting that "for sale" sign in your front yard, walk up to your home and pretend you've never seen it before.

- What do you notice first?
- How do you feel about what you see?
- Does the home seem inviting and well-maintained?
- Would you want to buy this house?

Your answer should be an enthusiastic yes!

First impressions count. In today's competitive housing market, every buyer is comparative shopping. A small investment in time and money can give your home a solid advantage over other properties.

By paying attention to the details, you can enhance the perceived value of your home, which will result in a quicker sale at a higher price.

Index

Accent Walls, 25
Accessorizing 30, 50
  Room Accessories, 33
  Wall Art, 30
Area Rugs, 22, 34
Balance
  Furniture Layouts, 36
  Lighting, 28
  Materials, 34
Clutter, 6, 19
Curb appeal, 3
Designer Tricks, 39
  Room Dimensions, 39
  Window Dimensions, 40
Depersonalizing, 14
Focal Points, 23, 50
  Art Arrangements, 25, 26
  Fireplaces, 24
  Window Views, 23
Furniture Layouts
  Arranging Tips, 20-22
  Diagonal Placement, 21

Harmony, 35
  Furniture Styles, 35
  Accessories, 35
  Balance, 35
  Scale, 37
  Symmetry, 37
Home Improvements, 42
Lighting, 27, 50
New Home Trends, 46
Neutralizing Décor, 12
Odors, 10
Online Home Shopping, 51
Painting Cabinets, 43
Pets, 15
Repairs, 8
Room Function, 19, 49
Staging
  Empty Houses, 45
  Do-It-Yourself, 16, 49
  Professional Stagers, 47
Traffic Flow, 18, 20, 36
Window Treatments, 13, 17, 27, 34, 44, 50

About the Author

Gloria Hander Lyons has channeled 30 years of training and hands-on experience in the areas of art, interior decorating, crafting and event planning into writing creative how-to books. Her books cover a wide range of topics including decorating your home, cooking, planning weddings and tea parties, crafting and self-publishing.

She has designed original craft projects featured in magazines, such as *Better Homes and Gardens, McCall's, Country Handcrafts* and *Crafts*.

Gloria teaches interior decorating, wedding planning and self-publishing classes at her local community college, as well as private classes and workshops.

Much to her family's delight, her kitchen is in non-stop test mode creating recipes for new cookbooks.

Visit her website for free decorating advice, event planning tips and tasty recipes at:

www.BlueSagePress.com

Other Books by Gloria Hander Lyons

- *Easy Microwave Desserts in a Mug*
- *Easy Microwave Desserts in a Mug for Kids*
- *No Rules—Just Fun Decorating*
- *Just Fun Decorating for Tweens & Teens*
- *Decorating Basics: For Men Only*
- *If Teapots Could Talk—Fun Ideas for Tea Parties*
- *The Super Bride's Guide for Dodging Wedding Pitfalls*
- *A Taste of Lavender: Delectable Treats with an Exotic Floral Flavor*
- *Lavender Sensations: Fragrant Herbs for Home & Bath*
- *Self-Publishing On a Budget: A Do-It-All-Yourself Guide*
- *Hand Over the Chocolate & No One Gets Hurt! A Chocolate-Lover's Cookbook*
- *The Secret Ingredient: Tasty Recipes with an Unusual Twist*

Ordering Information

To order additional copies of this book, send check or money order payable to:

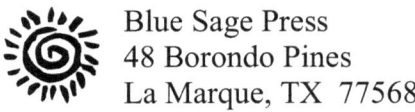
Blue Sage Press
48 Borondo Pines
La Marque, TX 77568

Cost for this edition is $6.95 plus $3.00 shipping and handling for the first book and $1.25 for each additional book shipped to the same address (U.S. currency only).

Texas residents add 8.25% sales tax to total order amount.

To pay by credit card or get a complete list of books written by Gloria Hander Lyons, visit our website at:

www.BlueSagePress.com.

www.ingramcontent.com/pod-product-compliance
Lightning Source LLC
Chambersburg PA
CBHW060724030426
42337CB00017B/2996